I0600560

In Fall

illustrated by
Marie Claude Monchaux

AUTHORS

Rochelle Nielsen-Barsuhn
    pages 7, 9, 11, 19, 21, 25, 29
Jane Belk Moncure
    pages 5, 13, 15, 17, 23, 27
Eleanor Hammond
    page 31

Library of Congress Cataloging in Publication Data

Nielsen-Barsuhn, Rochelle.
  Fall.

  Summary: A collection of poems describing the varied
aspects of autumn.
  1. Children's poetry, American.   2. Autumn—Juvenile
poetry. [1. Autumn—Poetry.   2. American poetry—
Collections] I. Moncure, Jane Belk.   II. Claude,
Marie, ill.   III. Title.
PS595.A89N54   1985   811'.54'08033   85-12817
ISBN 0-89565-329-X

Abdo & Daughters

In Fall

It's that back-to-school,
   football time
   of the year
when honking geese tell us,
"FALL IS HERE!"

Hello, Fall

Good-by, summer.
Good-by, swimming pool.
Hello, fall!
Hello, school!
Hello, football!
Hello, friends!
I'm glad fall is here
when summer ends.

Leaf Dance

If you were a leaf,
   would you dare
   leave your tree home
   to dance
   in the air?
I would.
I'd fall and whirl,
   waltz and swirl.
I'd help spruce up the ground
   in rust, gold, and brown.

Roly~Poly Pumpkins

How do you know
   when fall is here?
I'll give you a hint:
   fat pumpkins appear!
Orange and tubby, bright or pale —
   there are tons of pumpkins . . .
   all for sale.
But which one belongs
   by my door stop?
This butterscotch one
   with the pigtail top.

Apple Treats

It's apple time.
Come and see.
Come to the apple orchard
   with me.
Look at the apples, shiny
   and round —
    apples everywhere on the ground.
You can pick them up for an
   apple pie,
   or maybe for apple crisp.
But I like to eat them
   just like this —
      CRUNCH!

Wild Geese

In fall I watch
   the wild geese fly
   in wavy lines
   across the sky.
I say, "Good-by,"
   but I wish they
   would stay.
I wonder why
   geese fly
   so far away?

Cookout

When we have a cookout
   in the fall,
I like the log fire
   best of all.
It gets smoky,
   toasty, and
   sparkly bright —
   just right
   for roasting marshmallows
   at night.

Fall Hills

In winter the hills
    are white with snow.
In summer they turn to
    green.
But in fall they dress up
    in yellow
    and red
    and orange
    for Halloween!

Mr. Pumpkin

My pumpkin was just a pumpkin,
  but Dad said, "We'll fix that!"
He helped me give him
    some spooky eyes
    and a silly pumpkin hat.
Next we carved a funny nose
    and a one-tooth pumpkin grin.
He seemed to chuckle
    when we stuck
      a lighted candle in.

Boo! Guess Who?

Mostly I'm just me, myself,
  but on Halloween,
  I'm something else.
In my black-cat whiskers,
  tail, and feet,
  I knock at doors
  and shout,
  "Trick-or-treat!"

Frisky Chipmunks

Hi, frisky chipmunks,
  fat and furry.
Why are you in such
  a hurry
    to hide your seeds
    this cold fall day?
Who told you winter
  is on its way?

Busy Squirrel Friend

I wanted to make friends
   with a squirrel today,
   but she was far too busy
   storing acorns away.
Fall is here,
   and cold winter's ahead.
Soon Squirrel will crawl under cover
   and eat acorns in bed.

The Scarecrow

The farmer made a scarecrow
  and stuffed it full of straw.
He put it in the cornfield,
  but the crows laughed,
    "Haw-caw-caw."
One crow sat upon Scare-
  crow's hat.
He was not scared at all.
That scarecrow did not
  scare a single crow away
  all fall!

On Thanksgiving Day

I put rolls in a basket,
   crisp and warm,
   stirred the gravy,
   buttered the corn.
I watched the turkey
   cook golden brown.
I mashed potatoes
   while Mom sat down.
In fact,
   I was such a big help today
   that before we bowed our heads
     to pray,
Mom whispered,
"I'm thankful for *you.*"

Winter Is Coming

I walked down the lane
  past the maple tree,
and Postman wind
  brought a note to me —
a small yellow note
  from my friend the tree!
You call it a "leaf"
  just drifting down?
Why, it says, "Old Winter
  will soon be in town!"
So it's really a letter
  the tree sent down!

31